Welcome to Paris

Hello, my name is Pauline and I'm 8 years old.
The photographer up there is my brother Martin, he's 10.
We were both born in Paris.
It's the capital of France.
It's also the most visited city in the world.
Would you like to know why?
Then follow us! We're going to have lots of fun finding out.

To make reading easier for you,
difficult words have been highlighted in pink,
and are explained in the glossary p.59.

A few landmarks...

There are so many things to see and do in Paris. Here is a map so you can find your way around.
Let's get going!

La Défense

Quai Branly

Arc de Triomphe

Boulev

Champs-

Bois de Boulogne

16th

Eiffel Tower

Roland-Garros

Parc des Princes

the Seine

Invalides

15th

towards Versailles

La Villette

Montmartre

17th

18th

Canal Saint-Martin

19th

Moulin-Rouge

8th

9th

Opera

Buttes-Chaumont

Haussmann

Pompidou Centre

10th

Bd Haussmann

Concorde

2nd

20th

Louvre

3rd

1st

11th

Père Lachaise

Notre-Dame

4th

Orsay

Bastille

6th

5th

the Seine

12th

Parc du Luxembourg

Jardin des plantes

Montparnasse Tower

Bois de Vincennes

14th

13th

Chinatown

Let's speak french !

Would you like to discover the French language? Here are a few vocabulary words you can use to have fun learning French...your parents will definitely be impressed!

le petit-déjeuner
Breakfast

café
coffee

chocolat
hot chocolate

jus d'orange
orange juice

croissant
butter croissant

baguette
French bread

Puis-je avoir un  croissant s'il vous plaît ?
Can I have a butter croissant please?

Un peu de fromage ?
Would you like any cheese?

roquefort
Blue cheese

camembert
Soft cow's milk cheese

fromage de chèvre
Goat's cheese

Paname

No so long ago, Paris was not called Paris. It also has several nicknames. Let's have a closer look!

JEU

Right, let's not make this too easy...the names and descriptions have been mixed up a bit. Can you put them in the right order?

THE CITY OF LIGHTS ◯

LUTECIA ◯

PANAME ◯

A

B

C

This nickname appeared at the beginning of the 20th century. Probably because at the time, many Parisians used to wear a straw hat called a **"panama"**. It was made fashionable by workers who wore them to protect themselves against the sun while they were digging tunnels in... Panama (central America).

This expression dates back to the 17th century. Quite simply because Paris was the very first city to install **street lamps** in each of its streets. At the time, it was not to make the city look pretty, but to help stay on the look-out for the many crooks who would come and go in Paris.

The city was given this name in -50 BC. The Romans had taken over Gaul (old name for France). The name Paris came about in the year 310, in memory of the city's very first inhabitants, the **Parisii**.

So, did you find the answers? It is also said that Paris is the capital of fashion and food, and sometimes that it is the most beautiful city in the world.

I must say that's true!

Funny french snail

Paris has always been a really big city. So, in 1860, for people to find their way around and for better organisation, the city was split up into 20 large districts, called arrondissements in French. These districts still exist nowadays.

Have a look at the picture, they coil around the Seine river, and the city centre like a snail.
When you walk around the city, try and spot the street signs. They will always tell you which district you are in.

10.me ARR.t
RUE DE METZ

GAME Follow the clues to find out which district Martin is in!

- *The Seine river does not run through it*
- *It is a double-digit district*
- *It is smaller than the 17th district*
- *It is North of the 5th district*
- *It does not touch the 12th district*

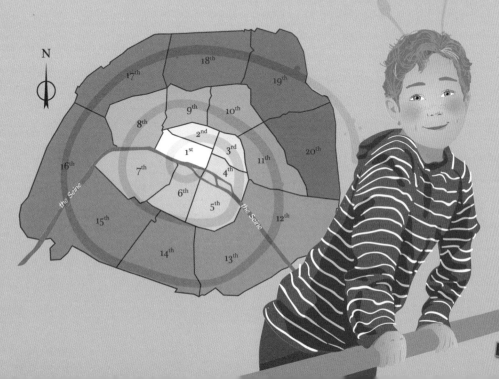

The Seine

Our famous river. It runs through the centre of Paris for 8 miles and splits the city into two halves: **the right bank** (to the North of the Seine) and **the left bank** (to the South). Luckily, 37 bridges were built for people to cross from one side to another.

The heart of Paris

The entire city of Paris was built **around the Seine river** years and years ago. That's because rivers are very practical for getting around and transporting goods. The very first inhabitants built their houses on the **île de la Cité** (City Island) because the Seine helped protect them against enemies.

And it has been the heart of the city ever since! All you need to do is count the number of monuments that line the Seine riverbanks. A large part of Paris' history can be told thanks to the river.

As you can see in the example, words can appear in any way possible, but WATCH OUT, each letter can only be used once.

GAME

TROCADÉRO, MUSÉE D'ORSAY, NOTRE-DAME, GRAND PALAIS, CONCIERGERIE, TOUR EIFFEL, LOUVRE, INVALIDES

In the grid below, find all these monuments located just next to the river.

G	T	O	U	O	T	R	E	D
R	A	N	R	N	S	U	M	A
C	O	D	E	I	E	E	T	M
L	N	P	I	F	F	D	R	E
O	C	A	N	V	E	O	O	C
U	I	L	A	A	L	R	S	A
V	E	S	I	L	■		A	D
R	R	G	E	I		Y	E
E	E	I	R	D	E	S	O	R

To discover Paris from the Seine river, nothing beats a ride on the famous Bateau-Mouche boats. We love them! In French, "mouche" means "fly", but these boats have nothing to do with flying. They were simple given that name because they were originally made in the Mouche district in the city of Lyon.

GAME

The Seine has three islands: the **île Saint-Louis**, the **île de la Cité** (where Notre-Dame stands) and a third one, often forgotten, the **île aux Cygnes** (Swan Island). It is only 12 yards long, but is renowned for its miniature replica of a very famous statue. Can you guess which one?

1

The statue of Neptune
(God of the sea)

Because a long time ago, the sea used to come right up to Paris.

2

The statue of Tintin

Because King Louis 14 already loved cartoons at the age of 5.

3

The statue of Liberty

In honour of Auguste Bartholdi, the Frenchman who created the statue of Liberty in New York.

Who would have thought?

From time to time, the Seine's water level rises enormously. This means it sometimes floods over onto Paris' embankments. Parisians therefore keep a close eye on the water by checking the statue of the Zouave, on the Alma bridge. Normally, his feet are dry. But if ever they disappear underwater, a flood is on the way. In 1910, during the last big flood, the Zouave statue had water right up to his shoulders!

Notre-Dame
de Paris

Does the name ring a bell? Of course it does. It's almost the same name as The Hunchback of Notre-Dame written by French author *Victor Hugo*.
The book tells the story of a gypsy girl, Esmeralda. The story revolves around Notre-Dame Cathedral in Paris during the 15th century. But you probably know much more about the cartoon, that tells the story of Quasimodo, *"the Hunchback of Notre-Dame"*.

Notre-Dame is the most visited monument in France, and therefore in Paris. **With 13 million visitors every year,** it even beats the Eiffel Tower. Mind you, this Gothic-style cathedral is quite simply magnificent.

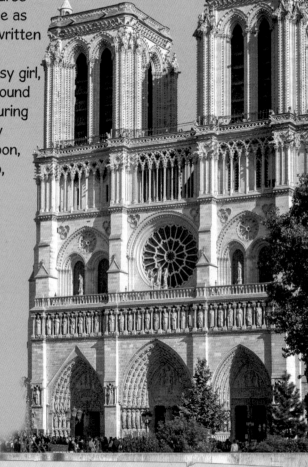

In 1163, Maurice de Sully, the bishop of Paris, took on a huge challenge: to build the most beautiful and largest cathedral in the world for the city of Paris. This enormous project lasted about 300 years! Sculptors, stonemasons, carpenters and bricklayers came from all over France to work on it.

Emmanuel
the bell

The South tower (the one on the right when you face the cathedral) is home to a huge tenor bell. This name is given to a big bell with a very deep bong. It weighs about 13 tonnes.
It is also called "Emmanuel". It is rung for major occasions like Christmas or Easter.

JEU Finish off the last 2 bells according to the logical sequence.

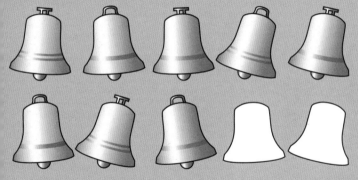

A devastating fire

A mighty fire broke out in the cathedral on 15 April 2019. Firefighters struggled for several hours against the flames and eventually managed to put out the fire. Unfortunately, most of the roof was destroyed and the 19th century spire* collapsed. Naturally, a prompt decision to rebuild Notre-Dame was made. The roof frame will need to be rebuilt. This task will take several years to complete.
* spire: Pointed end of a steeple and tower.

Watch out for the gargoyles

If you look up, you will see a lot of funny statues. They are gargoyles. They help get rid of rain water that runs through the gutters, and as they poke out the water does not dirty the cathedral walls.

The sculptors no doubt had a lot of fun designing these statues, they represent very strange animals or characters. They are even a little scary sometimes.

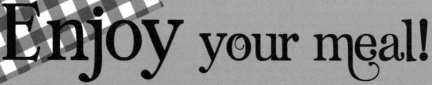

Enjoy your meal!

If you like good food, it's your lucky day.
Our city is mostly known for its brasseries (typical small French restaurants) with traditional decor. If you would like to try one, go to the **"Bouillon" Chartier**. This brasserie was opened in 1896! Why the name "Bouillon" (broth)? During the 19th century, this name was given to restaurants who served workers a meat dish and a broth for a very cheap price. Nowadays, at Chartier, meals are still very cheap (soups are only 1 euro).

Your bill will even be tallied directly with a pencil on your paper tablecloth. We find that quite amusing.

GAME

Can you help Martin choose a menu that will come to exactly 15 euros?

STARTERS
Soup of the day 1.00
Avocado in a prawn sauce 2.50
Leak salad 3.50

MAIN COURSES
Hamburger steak and chips 8.50
Black pudding and homemade mashed potatoes ... 9.00
Spaghetti Bolognese 8.50

CHEESE
Camembert 2.50
Goat's cheese 2.50

DESSERTS
Fresh pineapple 4.00
Pastry puff with whipped cream 3.50
Chestnut and vanilla pudding 3.00

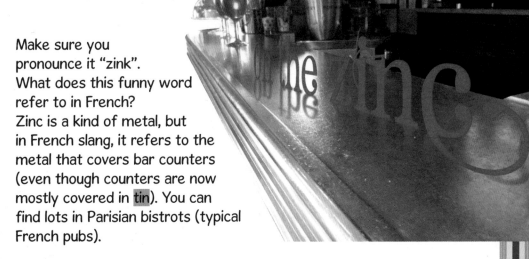

Make sure you pronounce it "zink". What does this funny word refer to in French? Zinc is a kind of metal, but in French slang, it refers to the metal that covers bar counters (even though counters are now mostly covered in tin). You can find lots in Parisian bistrots (typical French pubs).

GAME

The race is on at lunchtime here! Can you help the waitress finish her bills?

HAM SANDWICH €5.5

CROISSANT €1.5

ASSORTMENT OF 3 CHEESES €8.5

GLASS OF WINE €5

LEMONADE €3

WHITE COFFEE €3.5

1 croissant
1 coffee

1 ham sandwich
1 lemonade

1 assort. of cheese
1 glass of wine

The Louvre
The palace of all wonders

The most famous woman in the world is kept here, people go in through a pyramid and the former Kings of France used to live here. Welcome to the largest museum in the world!

A museum in a king's palace.

Before becoming a museum, the Louvre was a fortified castle built to fend off enemies.
Later on, King *Francis I* of France turned it into a huge and sumptuous residence for the Kings of France.
During the Revolution (1789-1799), the Louvre was transformed into a museum. When visiting it, do not forget you are actually in a former palace!

GAME

By adding up the numbers in the grid, discover the year in which the Louvre Pyramid was created.

A glass pyramid

No, it does not come from Egypt. It was created by *Ieoh Ming Pei*, a Chinese architect, to make it easier to spot the Louvre and the entrance to the museum. At night, with its thousands of glass rectangles, it looks like a big shining diamond.

The result of each square corresponds to the sum of the two squares beneath it.

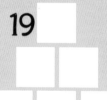
19

5
9
2 + 3 7 1

The Venus de Milo sculpture

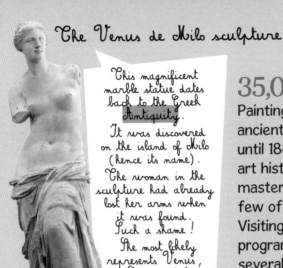

This magnificent marble statue dates back to the Greek Antiquity.

It was discovered on the island of Milo (hence its name).

The woman in the sculpture had already lost her arms when it was found! Such a shame!

The most likely represents Venus, the Goddess of love and beauty.

35,000 works of art!

Paintings, sculptures, trips through ancient Greece and Egypt...From Antiquity until 1848, you can discover a large part of art history. And of course admire incredible masterpieces. You probably already know a few of them.

Visiting the Louvre requires a jam-packed programme. You will probably need to visit it several times to see everything.

Luckily, entrance is free for children.

GAME

*There are so many people clustered around the star of the museum! It is quite difficult to catch a glimpse of the young lady painted by **Leonardo da Vinci**. By the way, do you know the name of this famous painting?*

the ☐☐☐☐☐☐☐☐☐☐

after the I

7th letter from the end

at the end

almost in the middle

N S O A I L

after the O

between the N and the L

A

3rd letter from the end

M

the 1st letter

A great idea *

The **Parisian metro** (underground train) was set up in 1900. Nowadays, 14 different lines and 135 miles of network allow you to travel from one side of Paris to the another. But what a mess it was to build!
Imagine having to drill gigantic tunnels and remove tonnes and tonnes of earth from underground.
Tunnels were even dug under the Seine.
The workers who contributed to its construction are no longer with us, but they can certainly be proud of their achievement: over 4 million travellers use the metro every day.

GAME *What is the best route for travelling from the **Montparnasse station** to the **Louvre Museum?***

> ** Good one Mister Bienvenüe !*
>
> *Everyone says he is the "father" of the Parisian metro. He was the creator of the very first network.*
>
> *That is why one of the stations was named after him at Montparnasse.*

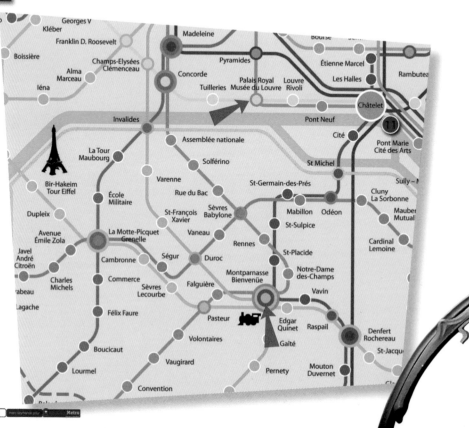

Do you know why the metro's platforms are covered in white tiles?

Quite simply because in 1900, there was never enough light down there (people could no longer read their newspapers). So white tiles were chosen

Aaaah! Much better!

Such a pretty metro!

Towards 1900, during the Art Nouveau period, the architect **Hector Guimard** designed the decorative entrances to metro stations. The most beautiful ones, with their glass roofs, look like dragonflies. There are still one or two remaining in Paris: the first is at **Porte Dauphine**, and the second at **Abesses**.

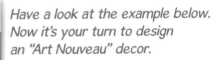

Have a look at the example below. Now it's your turn to design an "Art Nouveau" decor.

Hector Guimard was the main representative of the Art Nouveau period.

This artistic style gets its inspiration from nature. It uses flowers, leaves or animals as models... It is a decorative art often made of curved lines.

Look closely at this station entrance, it looks like the word "Métropolitain" is held up by two flower stems!

The Eiffel Tower

The Eiffel Tower is the capital's highest building. You can see it from practically anywhere. It is also Paris' real star. Every year, 7 million visitors hurry to climb up it and gaze out over the city. Let's have a quick tour of this incredible tower.

He won !

1889. *One hundred years after the French Revolution, Paris hosted a huge exhibition, to which all countries throughout the world were invited. Each country was allowed to present its achievements or inventions. In Paris, three years earlier, a huge competition was organised to determine which* masterpiece *would represent France. Amongst the 700 projects presented, the winner was: the* engineer **Gustave Eiffel** *(and his team). What was his idea? To build a huge iron tower!*

Incredible know-how

The construction started in 1887 and the tower was named after its inventor. It took 2 years, 2 months and 5 days to build. To do so, 15,000 pieces of iron were assembled and 2.5 million rivets were hammered in manually. What an acrobatic and meticulous challenge that was!

Once every 7 years, the Eiffel tower has a makeover. A whole year and 60 tonnes of paint are required to cover it from head to toe.

Up at the top, when the weather is clear, you can see up to _30 miles_ in every direction.

Can you hear me up there?

When the tower was first built, the plan was to take it down after 20 years. However, thanks to its great height, it quickly became very useful and was therefore kept. Indeed, in 1889, a weather station was set up right at the top. Aerials were then added, allowing messages to be sent during the first World War (1914–1918) and the very first radio shows were broadcast in 1921.

Total height

◻,0◻ _feet_

GAME

To find out how high the floors are, count the different coloured sticks, then write the results in the matching squares.

2nd floor

◻◻◻ _feet_

1st floor

◻◻◻ _feet_

N

E

W

S

Over here for all you sporty people.

The stairs start in the South pillar, and lead to the 1st and 2nd floor. You will have climbed 704 steps. Phew!

Fashion

No doubt about it, Paris is the capital of fashion. The **high fashion houses** have been set up here for a very long time now. High fashion means luxury clothing designed by great creators. They are extremely gifted. Every year and for each main season (autumn-winter and spring-summer), they design a new collection of clothes that will set the tone for future fashion. *Yves Saint-Laurent, Dior, Hermès, Jean-Paul Gaultier,* etc. These leading names in fashion make France very well-known throughout the world.

GAME

A   C   E   H   L   N   O

Follow the code using the models and discover the name of a famous designer who strongly influenced the world of fashion in France.

And for all you future fashion designers! 1900, 1930, 1950, 1960, 1970, 1980, 2010
Try and match each date with the right model. You can ask your mum or dad for some help !

Sweet treats from Paris

macaroons

Macaroons are so delicious. These little soft and round cakes made from almond paste, egg whites and sugar are famous here. They exist in any flavour and colour imaginable. In Paris, you can find them at *Ladurée* or *Pierre Hermé*. They are the kings of macaroons.

> Yummy, everything looks delicious over here. No wonder, you're just about to discover all our favourite treats. You should also know that in our city, bakers and pastry chefs are absolute champs !

Berthillon ice cream

If you walk around the *Île Saint-Louis*, don't hesitate to stop for ice cream at *Berthillon's*. He has been set up there since 1954. Vanilla, hazelnut, salted butter caramel or even gingerbread and lavender...you'll have a ball choosing your flavours.

the paris-brest

In 1910, a pastry chef called *Louis Durand* had a fun idea: he created a cake **in the shape of a bicycle wheel**. He wanted to glorify the Paris-Brest-Paris bicycle race. Since then, the pastry has come a long way.

A chance for baron Haussmann in Paris

The year was 1850. Paris' population was rapidly increasing, neighbourhoods were ageing and **epidemics** were appearing. Something had to be done. *Napoleon III* decided to call upon *Baron Haussmann*, who endeavoured to transform and embellish Paris. Actually, he just tore everything down.

He first replaced **20,000** **unsanitary** buildings with new and more modern ones. He also made room for very large boulevards.
If you walk along the *Boulevard des Capucines* for example, you can still see the results of this huge project.

Obviously, the Baron now has a boulevard named after him: *boulevard Haussmann*. It is located in the 8th and 9th district.

GAME *Can you find the ten cats hidden in this picture?*

Big ideas, big shops!

Paris is shopping paradise. Especially given the size of some of its shops! We have **Mr Boucicaut** to thank for that. In 1852, he had the idea of (greatly!) enlarging an old haberdashery shop, called **Bon Marché**. He had in actual fact just invented the largest shop in the world. Obviously, others wanted to follow suit. A few years later, **the Samaritaine, BHV, Printemps and Galeries Lafayette** opened their doors in the main Parisian boulevards.

These huge shops selling clothes, perfumes and home products still exist today. Their sumptuous decor has turned them into true monuments.

GAME *Circle the bears that have lost their twin.*

At Christmas, the windows of these big shops are decorated in an enchanting and magical way!

All in good fun!

Paris is theatre heaven.

There are approximately 200 of them spread out across the city.

Parisians enjoy going to **café-theatres** for entertainment. These small café-theatres host comedy shows and skits.

Of course, there are also larger Boulevard Theatres. Plays presented for audience entertainment are performed there. They stage funny misunderstandings drawn from our small day-to-day worries. In the 19th century, this kind of theatre was staged in the *Boulevard du Temple*, then in the main Parisian Boulevards.

Hence its name.

GAME

By deciphering the code, discover one of the most famous boulevard theatre playwrights.

A D E F U Y

top of
the Pops!

Every day in Paris, dozens of concerts are organised.
All types of musical styles are represented.
Obviously, the city is full of concert halls.
However, one of them is very special. It is called **the Olympia**.
People say it is a legendary music hall.

It is so famous that performers no longer *"sing at the Olympia"* but rather *"play the Olympia"*. **The Beatles, Jacques Brel, Édith Piaf, the Rolling Stones** or even **Lady Gaga** are examples of performers who *played the Olympia*.
Retiring artists often organise their last performances there too.

GAME *If you concentrate on the pink lines only, you will discover one of Edith Piaf's famous songs.*

Thanks for the shortcut!

In the early 1800s, a delightful invention spread out across Paris: **covered passages**.

What do you mean by covered passages? They were the 19ᵗʰ-century shopping centres. They wound through buildings, providing short-cuts from one boulevard to another. Parisians were delighted to be able to saunter around the shops quietly, sheltered from the bad weather and muddy streets. In these narrow streets, topped with glass roofs, a number of different shops were available: bookshops, delicatessens, jewellery shops, wine cellars, etc. The passages were even lit up and heated.

GAME

What is this young lady saying? Replace each letter with the one just before it in the alphabet. B=A, C=B, etc.

XBT UIJT IBU GSPN

UIF WJWJFOOF HBMLFSZ PS

UIF KPVGGSPZ QBTTBHF?

Until the middle of the 19ᵗʰ century, there were about 150 passages throughout Paris. There are still about 20 nowadays. They are true architectural wonders. Do not miss the Vivenne gallery and the Jouffroy passage...

On with the Music!

In around 1860, the Emperor **Napoleon III** started a huge competition.
He wanted the most magnificent opera to be built in Paris.
A young architect called **Charles Garnier** won the competition.
No wonder! The Opera, also called Palais Garnier, is a real masterpiece!
The show starts in the street itself. The façade, with its decorative sculptures,
mosaics and gold touches, dazzles an entire neighbourhood.
Even if you don't attend a show, don't miss out on the inside of the opera
house. You will enter into a marble and gold palace.

Colours all around

*Just like Chagall did,
draw what you feel when
you listen to your favourite music.*

*In the Italian-style theatre,
look up at the ceiling.
It has a gigantic painting on it,
created by the artist **Marc Chagall**.
In this fresco, Chagall attempted
to find the perfect colour
for certain types of music
or certain composers.
**Blue for instance
represents Mozart's
"Magic Flute".***

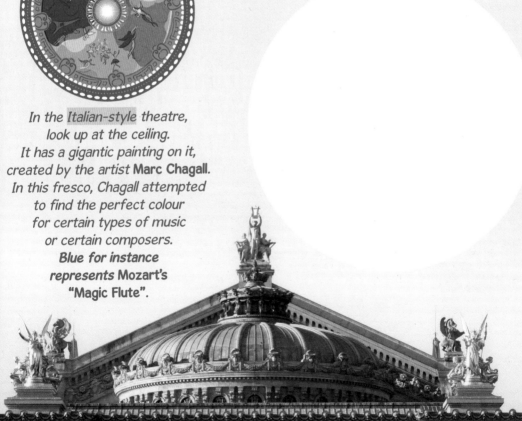

from the Grande Arche to the Louvre

Start off in the area of **La Défense**. This is where the Grande Arche stands. It was inaugurated in 1989 to celebrate the bicentenary of the French Revolution. Its architect wanted to create a "modern **Arc de Triomphe**". The result: a huge marble and steel cube whose sides each measure **360 feet**. Visitors who climb to the top get an amazing view over Paris' entire history. Monuments and centuries follow each other in a straight line for almost **5 miles**. From the Grande Arche to the Louvre pyramid, via the Champs Elysées... what a show!

GAME

Look at these perspectives, all the monuments' shadows have been placed one behind the other! Match the colours to the right monument.

Grande Arche

Arc de Triomphe

Grand Palais

Concorde

Tuileries

Louvre

Paris

the Concorde's obelisk

It is the oldest monument in Paris, but was not originally built here. It used to stand at the entrance of an Egyptian temple **over 3,000 years ago**.

Then, at the beginning of the 19th century, a Frenchman called *Champollion* discovered the secret of the **hieroglyphs***.

To show its appreciation, Egypt gave this large pointed column to France.
This huge present has been proudly standing in the middle of the Place de la Concorde since 1836.

* **Hieroglyphs** are a type of writing used by the Egyptians at the time of ancient Pharaohs. They represented small images or symbols.

GAME

Which Egyptian city does the Obelisk come from? To find out, read the letters hidden in the hieroglyphs from top to bottom.

on the Champs-Elysées

Everyone will tell you that the Champs-Elysées is "the most beautiful avenue in the world". It may be hard to imagine nowadays, but until the 18th century, **there were actually fields here**.

Nobody can leave Paris without having walked up the 1.2 miles of this lovely avenue, that links the Place de la Concorde with the Arc de Triomphe. If you have already played French Monopoly, you should know that this street is one of the most expensive in the city. This is why many companies, shops, cafés, cinemas and banks have set up here.

Watch out for these events

*The military procession happens here on **14 July every year**, to celebrate our National Day. Since 1975, the final stage of the **Tour de France** cycling competition also ends right here on the Champs-Elysées.*

What is this woman telling her husband? 1=A, 2=B, 3=C, etc.

GAME

20-5-14   13-15-18-5

19-8-15-16-19   1-14-4   9' 13

6-9-14-9-19-8-5-4

the Arc de triomphe

At the top of the avenue des Champs-Elysées sits a 50-metre high stone monument. Napoleon I decided to build it in 1806 to celebrate his victorious armies. Unfortunately for him, it was only finished in 1836, 15 years after his death.

Since 1920, the Arc de Triomphe has been home to the Tomb of the Unknown Soldier, symbolising the millions of French soldiers who died in combat during World War I (1914-1918).

You can climb the spiral staircase running up inside the monument, right out onto the terrace. The view over the city and the place de l'Étoile, over which the Arc de Triomphe reigns supreme, is amazing.

GAME

Add up all the numbers on the steps to find out how many there are in total.

The **Pont Alexandre III** (*Alexander III bridge*), the Decorative sculptures on the **Pont Neuf** and the Statue of Liberty on the **île des Cygnes**.

The Arc de Triomphe

Paris always leaves room for artists on its walls, that's street art for you !

MAKE ART NOT WAR

Your unavoidable guest during your strolls through Paris.

Pretending to be a king in the Tuileries gardens.

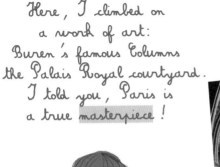

The **Mouzaïa** area looks just like a little village.

Here, I climbed on a work of art: Buren's famous Columns in the Palais Royal courtyard. I told you, Paris is a true masterpiece!

Second-hand book sellers set up their stands along the riverbanks over 300 years ago!

The Sainte-Chapelle: a gem of Gothic architecture and 600 m² of magnificent stained glass work.

The Panthéon was once a church and is now a monument to the glory of famous French people honoured by their country.

Orsay, a museum in a train station

Before becoming a museum, Orsay was a train station linking the towns located to the South-West of Paris. However, it grew too small. Its palace-like style was so beautiful that the city decided to turn it into a museum, exhibiting works of art dating back between 1848 to 1914. The old train station clocks were even kept.

On the front on the building, facing the Seine river, have fun counting the different towns served by the old station.

Impressive!

*The Musée d'Orsay and also the **Musée Marmottan** are renowned for the canvases painted **by great impressionists.***

These 19th-century artists preferred to paint the impression they got when looking at a landscape, rather than reality.

They expressed themselves using little dots of colour.

***Renoir, Manet** and **Monet** are world-renowned impressionist painters.*

*Here is part of **Claude Monet's "Impression, Sunrise".***

This painting gave its name to the impressionist movement.

Now it's your turn to imagine a sunset using little dots of colour.

* You can see the whole painting at the Marmottan museum

The Maison de Molière

No, this was not where **Molière** - one of the leading French playwrights -
lived. It is the nickname given to one of the most famous and oldest the
companies, the **"Comédie-Française"**. King **Louis XIV** created it
in 1680 as he loved theatre.

For over three centuries now, the **Comédie-Française**
has been performing French plays, especially those written
by **Molière**. To honour him, the **Comédie-Française**
is therefore also known as the **"Maison de Molière"**
(House of Molière).

Molière 1622-1673
(whose real name was Jean-Baptiste Poquelin)

Molière's plays were comedies.
Their goal was to entertain and amuse. They expose
the flaws and overindulgences
of the olden times in an amusing way.

For instance, "The Miser" presents a man
who refuses to ever spend any money.
It is still very funny, even nowadays.

GAME

*Here is a scene from "The Miser", one of Molière's plays.
Match the line with the right characters.*

- Did someone take money
from you?

- Yes, the rascal, and I'll have you
hanged if you don't give it back to me!

- Goodness me!
Do not treat him so harshl~
I can tell he is an honest m~

the Pompidou Centre

On 31 January 1977, the Parisian population discovered a rather strange construction in their city. It looked like a giant Meccano construction. This building is in fact a huge modern art museum called the *Pompidou Centre*. Its nickname is also *Beaubourg*. A real treat awaits you inside: there is a museum, a library, exhibition and cinema rooms and even a special area for kids.

The Pompidou Centre was named after Georges Pompidou, the French President from 1969 to 1974. It was his idea to build it in the first place. Unfortunately, he passed away before it was finished.

This building has nothing to hide. First of all, it is transparent. And the big multicoloured pipes are not just there for decoration. They also have an important role.

Electricity runs through the yellow pipes, air runs through the blue pipes and water runs through the green ones. The red ones are for movement within the building (stairs, lifts).

Air

Air

Air

Water

elevator

elevator

*electricity

the musée Grévin

Head to no. 10, boulevard Montmartre. This legendary museum, open since 1882, is home to over 200 celebrities from all over the world. They are made of wax, but look very lifelike. During your visit, you can wave to movie stars, shake hands with sports legends, spend some time with music idols or get your picture taken next to important historical figures. It should be pointed out that creating just one model is a long and artistic task that takes 6 months. Hats off to the artists!

Everyone has a part to play!

Over 15 artists work on creating each wax model. Sculptors, moulders, painters, implanters (hair), costumers, dental technicians, eyepiece prosthetists, props masters, decorators, etc.

Soprano posing for the sculptor Stéphane Barret – © Véronique Berecz

Leonardo **DiCaprio** ◯

Pablo **Picasso** ◯

Barack **Obama** ◯   Louis **XIV** ◯

Lionel **Messi** ◯

Marilyn **Monroe** ◯

Katy **Perry** ◯

Leonardo **da Vinci** ◯

cinema   music
sport   painting   history

You probably know who all these museum celebrities are. Can you colour them in to match their category?

© Grévin

They decorate Paris

the four caryatids

Sir Wallace's fountains

Feeling thirsty?
Look around for a Wallace fountain.
They date back to the end of the 19th century.
At the time, running and drinking water
could not be found everywhere.
In 1875, a very rich Englishman,
Sir Wallace, gave dozens of these
"drinking fountains' to the city of Paris.
They are made of cast iron and were painted
green so they blended in with the background.
The prettiest are adorned with
four **caryatids** (statues of women).
Nowadays, there are more than
100 Wallace fountains in Paris.

GAME

*Did you know that each of
the Wallace fountain caryatids
represent a human quality?
To find out what these qualities are,
follow the colour code.*

A B C H D E I K

L M N O P R S T Y

Mister Morris' columns

19th-century Paris. Mr Gabriel Morris was a printer specialised in posters for shows.
In 1868, the City of Paris granted him the right to build 450 cast iron columns, each 21 feet tall. These columns quickly became the best way for theatres to advertise their plays.

They were also used as storage space for brooms and street-cleaning equipment.
Nowadays, they advertise films, and some of them even turn!

GAME

7 differences have appeared between these two old show posters.

Montmartre
the eternal Village

Now it's time to wind your way up to the **Butte Montmartre** (Montmartre Hill). Granted, you will need to climb a few steps to reach the top of the hill. But you will not regret it when you get there: Paris turns into a quaint village!

Believe it or not, in the 19th century, Montmartre was covered in gardens, vines and windmills. Today, even though it has become very touristy, it has kept a countryside feeling to it. Vines still grow in the **rue Saint-Vincent**. Don't miss out!

GAME

Have a close look! 7 differences have slipped into these two scenes.

A favourite for Artists

In the 19th century, many painters and poets set up in Montmartre. They had a bohemian lifestyle. That means they lived quietly without worrying about the future.

Sacré-Cœur

After the Eiffel Tower, here is our city's second gem. People say it looks like a huge cream puff. But it is actually a basilica, which is a large church honoured by the Pope. It has towered over Paris since 1914. During its construction, people wanted it to be visible from anywhere in the city. Mission accomplished, thanks to its height and also to its pale colour. The **Sacré-Cœur** was built with **Château-Landon** stone, which actually becomes whiter with age!

Check it out!
Once inside the basilica, climb up to the dome.
You will get one of the most beautiful views of Paris.

Get some exercise!
If you climb up the Montmartre hill by foot, you will have walked up ⬜ steps, ⬜ feet high and ⬜ feet in total.

Add the right colours together

100
2
50
50
50
18
100
20
50
100
150
4

Otherwise, a funicular will take you to the top in 1 minute 30. It's quite fun too.

The Moulin-rouge

Still up and going!

Welcome to the most famous *cabaret* in the world! A cabaret?
It is a place where guests can have dinner whilst watching a show.
But this show is like no other. It has been at the foot of the Montmartre hill
since 1889! This windmill has never been active, but was an incredible place from
the very day it opened, with its gigantic dance floor and mirrors everywhere.
But what makes the *Moulin Rouge* even more successful is its famous dance:
the **French cancan**. The performers dance to lively and high-tempo music,
do the splits, lift their legs up as high as possible and (hush!) lift up their
petticoats too.

Yum

we love **Croque-Monsieur sandwiches**

This toasted sandwich is the star of French bistrots. It is said to have appeared for the first time in a Parisian café in 1910. Legend has it, it was named after an ogre-like bistrot manager. One day, having run out of baguette bread, he served a sandwich made with sliced bread. Stunned, one of his customers asked what was in it. As a joke, the manager answered: "Toasted you of course!"

The recipe *(for 1 toasted sandwich)*

2 thick slices of white bread

1 slice of ham.

A large handful of grated cheese

A dab of butter (for cooking)

❶ Take a slice of bread and cover it with the slice of ham, folded in half. ❷ Sprinkle the grated cheese over it. ❸ Cover with the second slice of bread. ❹ In a frying pan (get some help from an adult), melt the butter without letting it burn. ❺ Place the sandwich in the frying pan, cook on each side until golden.

there you have it! enjoy!
You can eat your sandwich with a green salad on the side if you like.

ADD A LITTLE SOMETHING! *To make a **croque-madame** sandwich, simply add a fried egg on top of your **croque-monsieur**.*

Auguste Rodin

Auguste Rodin was born in Paris in 1840, and is one of the most famous French sculptors. **His fascination with drawing** started at a very early age. At the age of 15, he discovered the art of sculpting and became fascinated in the human body, which he studied carefully. This is why his human figures are extremely **strong and highly expressive**.
The *Biron hotel*, where he used to live, has now become a museum where you can discover a large number of his works of art, such as ***"The Kiss"***.

"The Thinker", his most famous sculpture, stands in meditation in the Biron hotel gardens. Originally, this statue only measured 21 inches and was supposed to be part of a huge doorway. But **Rodin** *finally decided to make it into an individual work of art, that now measures close to 6 feet. This game will explain the stages for creating such an incredible work of art.*

GAME

Put the stages in the right order using numbers, then match them with the corresponding statue.

◯ The model is melted down in <u>bronze</u>.

◯ The sculptor tests and designs his models using <u>terracotta</u>.

◯ The selected model is then made to scale using <u>plaster</u>.

Fun with science

If you fancy playing chemists
or becoming a famous scientist,
head towards the *Cité des sciences*
or the *Palais de la découverte**.
Science can be discovered in a fun way there,
and visitors are invited to participate in loads
of surprising experiments.

In the incredible city of science or palace
of discoveries, you can travel through space,
pretend to be an ant, have a race with
a skeleton or understand the logic of
mathematics. Not to worry, there will be no
tests or unexpected quizzes at the end!

** The Palais de la découverte is currently closed
for works. Reopening planned in 2024.*

GAME

*Ready to perform an experiment
in your kitchen? Follow these
steps and watch closely...*

What you will need...

3 different food colourings (or ink)

milk

washing-up liquid

a cotton bud

1 soup bowl

Step 1

Pour a little milk into the bowl

Step 2

Drip a few drops of colouring in the middle

Step 3

Dip the cotton bud into the washing-up liquid, then plunge it into the centre of the coloured areas and see what happens.
Magic? No, chemistry!

*Pauline is doing
an electrostatics
experiment at
the **Palais de la
Découverte**.
Draw her hair
standing up on end!*

GAME

47

Welcome to the Quai Branly

Africa, the Americas, Asia, Oceania. It's time for a trip around the four corners of the Earth. Here is the Quai Branly - Jacques Chirac museum. Its name comes from its location (on the Seine riverbank, not far from the Eiffel Tower).

There are 3,000 exhibited objects, such as masks from around the world. They are not necessarily used to dress-up. They are artistic objects used to help you understand the rites or traditions respected in far-off countries.

During your visit, you will learn that these masks each have a specific function: to cure illnesses, to help find food, to celebrate weddings or chase evil spirits away after death.

*These masks from **Sri Lanka**, with their bulging eyes, do not look very friendly at all!*

Quite on the contrary, they are used to chase Evil away (when people are sick for instance).

Sri Lanka is a country located to the South of India.

Now it's your turn to imagine the most ferocious mask possible to chase away Evil forces!

48

the whole World

All throughout the 20th century, and still today, millions of foreigners have settled in Paris in search of work or a better life.

(CC Mbzt)

The Grand Mosque of Paris

That is why, when you walk around certain areas in Paris, you may feel like you are walking in different countries **around the world**.
In the 13th district, you can wander around the largest Chinese district in Europe. We call it **Chinatown**.
A little more to the North, the *Goutte d'Or* (Golden Drop) district makes you feel like you are in Africa. In the 5th district, Muslims can pray in France's largest mosque.
Get ready to travel!

With which area of the world can you associate these objects seen in Paris?

GAME

North Africa

Sub-Saharan Africa

China

Russia

Matryoshka doll

Lantern

Tagine

Djembe

do you fancy a walk in the woods?

No, there are not only large boulevards and monuments in Paris. There is actually quite a lot of greenery.
Over 400 parks and gardensare spread out across the city.
To get some fresh air, go for a bike ride, a boat ride or just for a picnic, you will be spoiled for choice. You may even come face to face with a number of animals.
Today, we are heading to the Luxembourg gardens. You can go pony-riding, play tennis or even watch a Punch-and-Judy show. My sister and I love renting the little sailing boats that we can push around the lake with a stick. They have been around since 1881.

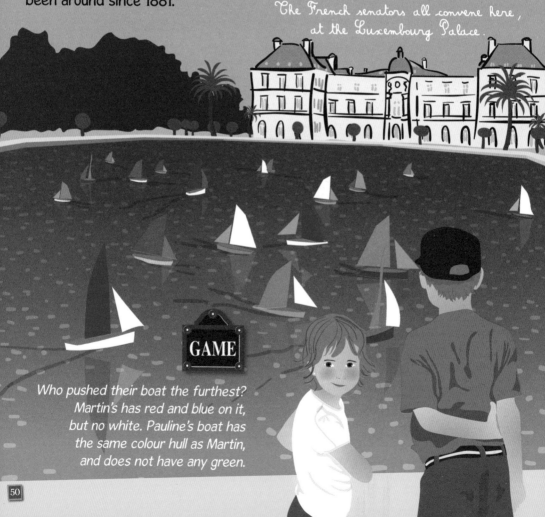

The French senators all convene here, at the Luxembourg Palace.

GAME

Who pushed their boat the furthest? Martin's has red and blue on it, but no white. Pauline's boat has the same colour hull as Martin, and does not have any green.

GAME

Put the pictures back in the right order.

The **Bois de Vincennes** or **Bois de Boulogne** make you feel like you are in a real forest. There are oak trees everywhere.
Pauline and I love the **Jardin d'Acclimatation** in the **Bois de Boulogne**: the attractions, the petting farm, discovery gardens.
Do not forget the zoos! Yes, zoos in Paris!
The zoo at Vincennes has just been fully revamped, and the **Jardin des Plantes** one is quite simply the oldest zoo in the world!
Dad prefers walking through the Tuileries gardens to look at the sculptures.

Just a few steps away from the woods, the Château de Vincennes, with its enormous dungeon (164 ft high!), is one of the largest and best-preserved castles in Europe.
It is well worth a visit.

what a gem!

Make way for luxury!

Here, in Place Vendôme, you will find all the city's prestigious jewellery shops: **Chaumet, Boucheron, Cartier, Van Cleef & Arpels, etc.** These leading names in the fine jewellery industry illuminate the beautiful square, surrounded by a number of private hotels dating back to the 18th century.

Other famous names have also settled there: the Ritz (a famous 5-star hotel, at no.15) and the Ministry of Justice (at no.11). In the centre of the square, an unmissable column stands 145 feet tall: the Vendôme column. Napoleon 1st had it built to commemorate the Battle of Austerlitz.

Of course, he is the one standing at the top of the column.

JEU

The names of these four precious stones were mixed up.

Can you put them back in the right order?

Dia -phire   *Ru* -mond

Eme -by   *Sap* -rald

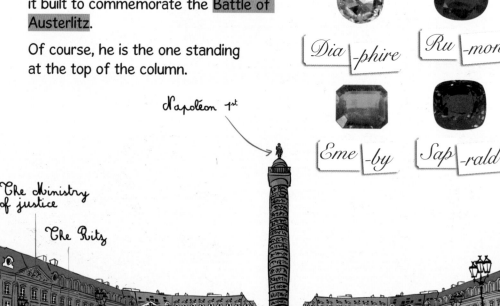

Napoléon 1st

The Ministry of justice

The Ritz

what lies beneath Paris

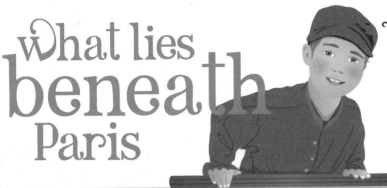

There are a number of surprising things under our city's streets.
We can even go and visit them.
Follow me!

the sewer systems

Walking around the sewer systems? Yuck! Come on, it's actually really interesting. Here, underground, the dirty water is collected and taken to cleaning stations. It is just like another city beneath the city. **Each street in Paris has its own sewer named after it.** The building numbers are even written down so you cannot get lost. 300 sewage workers supervise this maze that spreads out over more than 1,500 miles. This kind of job is often passed down from father to son.

GAME This sewage worker is lost, can you help him find his way back?

the catacombs

Since the end of the 18th century, millions of skulls and shin-bones have been piling up in these underground quarries.
*At the time, all the cemeteries were full, so people decided to transfer century-old bones to this place. The bones of **Jean de La Fontaine**, a famous French poet, are said to be here. So, are you up for a tour? No scaredy-cats allowed!*

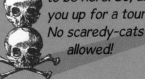

the palace of Versailles

Since 1979, the palace of Versailles has been classifi as a Unesco World Heritage site.

Here we are, 12 miles away from Paris. But it is worth it! The palace of Versailles is one of the most magnificent palaces in the world. *Louis XIV* had it built in the 1660's. He had a taste for glory and luxury.

The palace was designed by the architect Le Vau. It spreads out over 41 square miles and has over 2,000 rooms, including the very famous **Hall of Mirrors.**

This long and stunning hall measures 240 feet and is fitted with 357 mirrors! The decor has not changed since the King lived there, and just like anyone who ever visited him, you will no doubt be highly impressed.

Who said I enjoyed luxury?

Louis XIV's emblem on the palace's golden gates

The Hall of Mirrors

GAME

Do you what other name was given to King Louis XIV? Discover it by following the arrows.

one square down

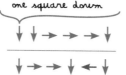

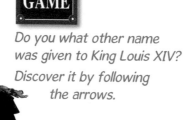

Start

T	B	A	U	D	V	O
H	E	-	S	E	R	N
G	A	L	U	A	A	B
L	O	E	N	-	K	C
A	R	R	A	N	I	H
C	A	I	A	G	T	A
E	S	E	A	L	E	A

Roland Garros

on earth...

We absolutely love tennis.
We are quite lucky to be living in Paris.
Every year, one of the four biggest tour-
naments in the world is held here. It is one
of the Grand Slam titles (the others are
in New York, London and Melbourne). In
Paris, the best players in the world face
each other at the **Roland Garros** stadium.
They play on **clay courts**. They have a
lovely orange colour, and are covered in a
thin layer of powdered bricks. This helps
make the ball more visible and allows the
players to slide and catch it. Well played!

...and up in the sky

Roland Garros was a French pilot. In 1913, he was the first to cross the Mediterranean Sea by plane. The tennis stadium was named after him in commemoration.

GAME

*No, Roland Garros' plane was not a pushchair!
Connect the dots to see what his machine really looked like.*

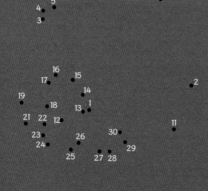

Saint-martin canal

We love going for walks along this canal. We can really take it easy. We have so much fun climbing up on the footbridges and watching the boats or barges navigate up the canal to *La Villette*. They depart from Paris' port (not joking), called the *Bassin de l'Arsenal*. They must cover almost 3 miles (just over 1 mile of which is underground), overcome a difference in height of 82 feet and cross 9 **locks**.

What are locks exactly?

They are like little dams, where water levels can be changed. This way, boats can cross from one level to another.

The boat asks for the gates to be opened.

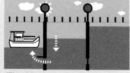

The 1st gate opens. The water flows in.

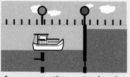

As soon as the water level has evened out, the boat goes through.

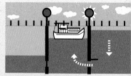

The 1st gate closes. The 2nd gate opens.

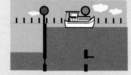

The water level evens out, the boat goes through.

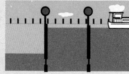

The 2nd gate closes.

Lights, camera, action!

Paris has been the backdrop for hundreds of films. Some have even become world-famous, even the old ones. *Les Enfants du Paradis* (Children of Paradise) or *Hôtel du Nord* are for example two masterpieces that were in cinemas when your grandma or grandpa were just babies!

HÔTEL DU NORD (1938)

*The film is set in a quaint hotel located along the Saint-Martin canal. The most famous scene takes place on a nearby footbridge. The leading actress speaks her main line there, which ended up becoming very famous: **"Atmosphere, atmosphere...do you really think I look like atmosphere?"***

Nowadays, the actual Hôtel du Nord still exists, but it was turned into a restaurant. Its façade takes us back to the olden days.

GAME *Here is the actress who had the leading role in both these great French films. Do not forget her name, she is truly legendary!*

A E L R T Y

Oh là ! là ! French words in english

Look at these words, they may ring a bell in English.
But they are actually French!

APÉRITIF
(cocktail)

PETITS FOURS
(sweet treats)

AU GRATIN
(with melted cheese)

À LA CARTE
(not in a set menu)

CHAISE LONGUE
(deck chair)

PINCE-NEZ
(nose clip)

COUP DE FOUDRE
(love at first sight)

BON VOYAGE
(enjoy your trip)

BILLET DOUX
(love letter)

the glossary

Antiquity

Antiquity
The oldest period in terms of human civilizations. It goes from the beginning of History until the fall of the Roman Empire (in about 476 AC).

Battle of Austerlitz
It took place in 1805 in what is currently the Czech Republic. Napoleon 1st won this battle.

Electrostatics
The study of static electricity. Static electricity refers to the strength transferred from one electrically-charged object to another object or body.

Engineer
A person who manages construction work and does research.

Epidemic
An illness that affects a very large number of people at the same time and in the same place.

Fine jewellery
The art of producing jewellery using precious materials (gold, silver).

Gothic-style
Gothic architecture was very common between the 12th and the 16th centuries, especially for the construction of cathedrals. It is characterised by its pretty vaults and large windows.

Haberdashery
A shop specialised in sewing, thread and buttons.

Italian-style
An enclosed Italian-style theatre is a round theatre. It has several floors, each with balconies.

Legendary
Mythical.

Line
In theatre or cinema, a line is a sentence or text spoken by an actor to another character.

Masterpiece
A remarkable, perfect piece of work.

Mosque
Place where Muslims pray.

Music hall
A hall for variety shows.

Muslim
A person who practices Mahomet's religion, Islam.

Rite
Custom, habit.

Rivet
A type of nail.

Saunter
To take your time, wander around without hurrying.

Tin
A slightly grey metal that is easy to shape.

Unesco World Heritage site
Unesco (United Nations Educational, Scientific and Cultural Organization) has established a list of 900 cultural or natural sites it considers should be either known or protected, that have great importance on an international level.
For instance, Stonehenge in England, and the Grand Canyon in the United States.

Unsanitary
Unhealthy.

Zouave
A French army soldier serving in Africa.

Music hall

Answers

Page 8:
The City of Lights: B
Paname: A
Lutecia: C

Page 9:
Martin is in the 10th district.

Page 11:
3 - It is the statue of Liberty.

Page 13:

Page 10:

G T O U O T R E D
R A N R N S U M A
C O D E L E E T M
L N P I F E D R E
O C A N V E O O C
U I L A A U R S A
V E S I L L A D Y
R R G E I Y E E
E E I R D E S O R

Page 16:
The pyramid dates back to 1989

40 49
15 25 24
5 10 15 9
2 3 7 8 1

Page 14:
For example:

soup of the day	1.00
spaghetti bolognese	8.50
camembert	2.50
chestnut and vanilla pudding	3.00
	15.00

Page 17:
The Mona Lisa.
It has 15,000 visitors every day!

Page 21:
1 2 3 6 7 8
1st floor: 187 feet
2nd floor: 377 feet
Total height: 1,062 feet

Page 15:

Page 8:

Page 22:
Coco Chanel

1900   1930   1950   1960   1970   1980   2010

Page 24:

Page 25:

Page 28:
WAS THIS HAT FROM THE VIVIENNE GALLERY OR THE JOUFFROY PASSAGE?

Page 26:
FEYDEAU

Page 27:
LA VIE EN ROSE

Page 30:
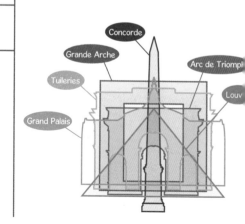

Concorde
Grande Arche
Tuileries
Grand Palais
Arc de Triomphe
Louvre

Page 31:
LUXOR

Page 32:
TEN MORE SHOPS AND I'M FINISHED

Page 33: 284 steps
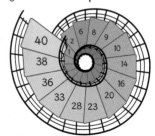

40
38
36
33
28 23
2 6 8 9
10
14
16
20

Page 37:

- Did someone take money from you?

- Yes, the rascal, and I'll have you hanged if you don't give it back to me!

- Goodness me! Do not treat him so harshly. I can tell he is an honest man.

Page 39:

Leonardo DiCaprio

Pablo Picasso

Barack Obama

Louis XIV

Lionel Messi

Marilyn Monroe

Katy Perry

Leonardo da Vinci

Page 40:

KINDNESS,
SIMPLICITY,
CHARITY,
SOBRIETY

Page 41:

théâtre Daunou
7, rue Daunou - métro Opéra - OPÉ : 64.50-28.75

Ah! les belles bacchantes

spectacle frétillant en 2 parties
de Robert Dhéry
Francis Blanche et Gérard Calvi

Page 42:

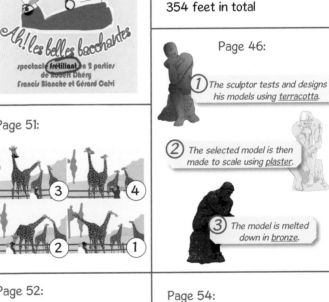

Page 43:
222 steps
118 feet high
354 feet in total

Page 46:

The sculptor tests and designs his models using terracotta.

The selected model is then made to scale using plaster.

The model is melted down in bronze.

Page 49:

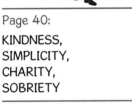

China

Russia

North
Africa

Sub-Saharan
Africa

Page 50:

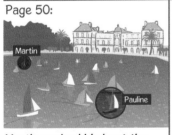

Martin

Pauline

Martin pushed his boat the furthest.

Page 51:

3   4

2   1

Page 53:

Page 52:

Diamond   Ruby

Emerald   Sapphire

Page 54:
The Sun King

Page 57:

ARLETTY

DISCOVER FRANCE IN A FUN WAY!

A collection of **PLAYFUL BOOKS** to encourage children to become acquainted with french culture.

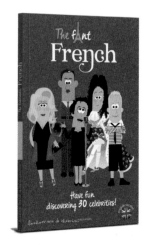

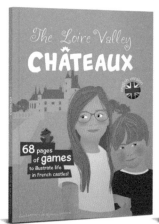

Authors: Stéphanie and Hugues Bioret, Julie Godefroy

Illustrations: Stéphanie Bioret, Julie Godefroy

Photo credits: ©Adobe Stock - ©iStock - Rémi Jouan *Paris Opera house (p.29)* - Nicolas Sanchez *Clockand Musée d'Orsay (p.37)* Stéphanie and Hugues Bioret

Acknowledgements: Mr Fabien de Sylvestre *(illustration of 17th-century Paris)*, Bouillon Chartier, Cram *(for its original design of the Parisian metro)*, Domitille Bioret, Guy Bioret, our little game "testers", Martin, Angèle and Jules...

© Bonhomme de Chemin Publications, 2022/Copyright

CONTACT:
tel. +33 (0)6 13 54 19 80
bonhommedechemin@orange.fr
www.bonhommedechemin.fr

In compliance with law no.49956 from 16 July 1949 regarding publications for children

ISBN: 979-10-92714-02-9

Raynaud printing company, France - Printed on PEFC paper
Printing completed in july 2022
Legal submission: February 2014